# 50 French Pastries to Master at Home

By: Kelly Johnson

# Table of Contents

- Croissant
- Pain au Chocolat
- Kouign-Amann
- Brioche à Tête
- Chausson aux Pommes
- Palmier
- Financier
- Madeleine
- Canelé
- Tarte Tatin
- Paris-Brest
- Mille-Feuille
- Opéra Cake
- Saint-Honoré
- Religieuse
- Éclair
- Chouquette
- Profiterole
- Clafoutis
- Crêpes Suzette
- Galette des Rois
- Pithivier
- Tarte au Citron Meringuée
- Tarte aux Fraises
- Tarte aux Pommes
- Macaron
- Baba au Rhum
- Gâteau Basque
- Pain d'Épices
- Gâteau Opéra
- Sablé Breton
- Tarte Tropézienne
- Mont Blanc
- Fraisier
- Croustade

- Soufflé au Chocolat
- Flan Parisien
- Charlotte aux Fraises
- Bûche de Noël
- Puits d'Amour
- Gâteau Mille-Crêpes
- Merveilleux
- Nougat de Montélimar
- Quatre-Quarts
- Pain aux Raisins
- Beignet
- Gâteau Breton
- Fougasse Sucrée
- Gâteau de Savoie
- Tourtière

## Croissant

(A flaky, buttery pastry with delicate layers.)

**Ingredients:**

- 4 cups all-purpose flour
- ¼ cup sugar
- 2 tsp salt
- 1 tbsp active dry yeast
- 1 ¼ cups whole milk, warmed
- 1 cup unsalted butter, cold
- 1 egg (for egg wash)

**Instructions:**

1. Mix flour, sugar, salt, and yeast. Add warm milk and knead into a dough.
2. Chill for 2 hours, then roll out and incorporate butter using a letter-fold method.
3. Fold and chill the dough three times, rolling it out each time.
4. Roll into a large rectangle, cut into triangles, and roll each into a croissant shape.
5. Proof for 2 hours, brush with egg wash, and bake at 375°F (190°C) for 18-20 minutes.

## Pain au Chocolat

(Flaky pastry filled with rich chocolate.)

**Ingredients:**

- 1 batch croissant dough
- 4 oz dark chocolate, cut into sticks
- 1 egg (for egg wash)

**Instructions:**

1. Roll out croissant dough and cut into rectangles.
2. Place a chocolate stick near one edge and roll tightly.
3. Proof for 2 hours, brush with egg wash, and bake at 375°F (190°C) for 18-20 minutes.

## Kouign-Amann

(A caramelized, buttery pastry from Brittany.)

**Ingredients:**

- 2 ½ cups all-purpose flour
- 1 ¼ tsp salt
- 1 tbsp sugar
- 1 tsp yeast
- ¾ cup water, warm
- 1 cup unsalted butter, cold
- ½ cup sugar (for layering)

**Instructions:**

1. Mix flour, salt, sugar, yeast, and warm water into a dough.
2. Chill for 2 hours, then roll out and incorporate butter using a letter-fold method.
3. Repeat folding three times, dusting with sugar before each fold.
4. Roll out, cut into squares, and fold the corners toward the center.
5. Proof for 1 hour, then bake at 400°F (200°C) for 25-30 minutes.

## Brioche à Tête

(A rich, buttery French bread with a distinctive round top.)

**Ingredients:**

- 2 ½ cups all-purpose flour
- ¼ cup sugar
- 1 tsp salt
- 1 tbsp active dry yeast
- 3 eggs
- ½ cup butter, softened
- ¼ cup milk
- 1 egg yolk (for egg wash)

**Instructions:**

1. Mix flour, sugar, salt, and yeast. Add eggs and milk, kneading until smooth.
2. Knead in butter, then chill for 4 hours.
3. Divide into small balls, place in greased brioche molds, and top with a small dough ball.
4. Proof for 2 hours, brush with egg wash, and bake at 375°F (190°C) for 20 minutes.

**Chausson aux Pommes**

(A flaky apple turnover with a buttery crust.)

**Ingredients:**

- 1 sheet puff pastry
- 2 apples, peeled and diced
- 2 tbsp sugar
- ½ tsp cinnamon
- 1 tbsp butter
- 1 egg (for egg wash)

**Instructions:**

1. Cook apples with sugar, cinnamon, and butter until soft.
2. Cut puff pastry into circles, place apple filling on one half, and fold over.
3. Seal the edges, brush with egg wash, and bake at 375°F (190°C) for 20 minutes.

## Palmier

(Crisp, caramelized puff pastry cookies.)

**Ingredients:**

- 1 sheet puff pastry
- ½ cup sugar

**Instructions:**

1. Roll out puff pastry and sprinkle with sugar.
2. Fold both edges toward the center, then fold in half again.
3. Slice into ½-inch pieces and bake at 400°F (200°C) for 15 minutes.

## Financier

(A small almond cake with a buttery, golden crust.)

**Ingredients:**

- ½ cup butter, melted
- ½ cup almond flour
- ⅓ cup powdered sugar
- ¼ cup all-purpose flour
- 3 egg whites
- ½ tsp vanilla extract

**Instructions:**

1. Mix almond flour, sugar, and flour.
2. Whisk in egg whites and vanilla, then stir in melted butter.
3. Pour into molds and bake at 375°F (190°C) for 15 minutes.

## Madeleine

(Soft, shell-shaped sponge cakes.)

**Ingredients:**

- ½ cup butter, melted
- ½ cup sugar
- 2 eggs
- ¾ cup all-purpose flour
- ½ tsp baking powder
- 1 tsp vanilla extract

**Instructions:**

1. Beat eggs and sugar until pale. Stir in vanilla.
2. Fold in flour, baking powder, and melted butter.
3. Chill batter for 1 hour, then pour into greased madeleine molds.
4. Bake at 375°F (190°C) for 10-12 minutes.

## Canelé

(A custardy pastry with a caramelized crust.)

**Ingredients:**

- 2 cups milk
- 1 tbsp butter
- ¾ cup sugar
- 1 cup flour
- 2 egg yolks + 1 whole egg
- 2 tbsp rum
- 1 tsp vanilla extract

**Instructions:**

1. Heat milk and butter until warm.
2. Whisk eggs, sugar, and flour, then stir in warm milk.
3. Add vanilla and rum, then chill batter for 24 hours.
4. Pour into greased canelé molds and bake at 450°F (230°C) for 10 minutes, then at 375°F (190°C) for 50 minutes.

**Tarte Tatin**

(A caramelized upside-down apple tart.)

**Ingredients:**

- 4 apples, peeled and sliced
- ½ cup sugar
- ¼ cup butter
- 1 sheet puff pastry

**Instructions:**

1. Melt butter and sugar in a pan until caramelized.
2. Add apples and cook until soft.
3. Place puff pastry over the apples, tuck edges, and bake at 375°F (190°C) for 30 minutes.
4. Flip upside down before serving.

# Paris-Brest

(A ring-shaped choux pastry filled with praline-flavored cream.)

**Ingredients:**

**For the choux pastry:**

- ½ cup water
- ½ cup milk
- ½ cup butter
- 1 tsp sugar
- ½ tsp salt
- 1 cup all-purpose flour
- 4 eggs
- ¼ cup sliced almonds (for topping)
- 1 egg (for egg wash)

**For the praline cream:**

- 1 cup whole milk
- 3 egg yolks
- ¼ cup sugar
- 2 tbsp cornstarch
- ½ cup praline paste
- 1 cup heavy cream

**Instructions:**

1. Preheat oven to 375°F (190°C).
2. Heat water, milk, butter, sugar, and salt in a saucepan until boiling.
3. Add flour and mix until dough forms. Remove from heat and mix in eggs one at a time.
4. Pipe into a ring on parchment paper, brush with egg wash, and top with sliced almonds.
5. Bake for 30-35 minutes until golden.
6. For the filling, heat milk. Whisk egg yolks, sugar, and cornstarch, then mix in hot milk. Cook until thick, then stir in praline paste. Cool and fold in whipped cream.
7. Slice the pastry ring and fill with praline cream.

## Mille-Feuille

(A layered pastry with crisp puff pastry and pastry cream.)

**Ingredients:**

- 1 sheet puff pastry
- 2 cups pastry cream
- ½ cup powdered sugar

**Instructions:**

1. Preheat oven to 375°F (190°C).
2. Roll out puff pastry, prick with a fork, and bake between two baking sheets for 20 minutes.
3. Once cooled, cut into three equal rectangles.
4. Layer with pastry cream, stacking the sheets.
5. Dust with powdered sugar and serve.

# Opéra Cake

(A layered almond sponge cake with coffee buttercream and chocolate ganache.)

**Ingredients:**

**For the almond sponge cake:**

- ½ cup almond flour
- ½ cup sugar
- ¼ cup all-purpose flour
- 3 eggs
- 2 egg whites
- 2 tbsp melted butter

**For the coffee buttercream:**

- ½ cup butter
- 1 cup powdered sugar
- 2 tbsp strong coffee

**For the chocolate ganache:**

- ½ cup heavy cream
- ½ cup dark chocolate

**Instructions:**

1. Preheat oven to 375°F (190°C). Mix almond flour, sugar, and eggs. Fold in whipped egg whites, then melted butter. Bake in a thin layer for 10 minutes.
2. Make coffee buttercream by whipping butter, powdered sugar, and coffee.
3. Heat cream, pour over chocolate, and stir until smooth.
4. Layer cake with buttercream and ganache, finishing with ganache on top.

## Saint-Honoré

(A caramelized puff pastry with cream-filled choux and whipped cream.)

**Ingredients:**

- 1 sheet puff pastry
- 1 batch choux pastry (see Paris-Brest)
- 1 cup pastry cream
- 1 cup whipped cream
- ½ cup caramelized sugar

**Instructions:**

1. Preheat oven to 375°F (190°C). Bake puff pastry into a round base.
2. Pipe and bake small choux pastry puffs.
3. Fill puffs with pastry cream and dip in caramel.
4. Arrange on the puff pastry base and pipe whipped cream in the center.

## Religieuse

(A double-layered choux pastry with pastry cream and chocolate glaze.)

**Ingredients:**

- 1 batch choux pastry
- 1 cup pastry cream
- ½ cup chocolate ganache

**Instructions:**

1. Pipe and bake small and large choux puffs.
2. Fill with pastry cream.
3. Dip tops in chocolate ganache and stack the smaller choux onto the larger one.

## Éclair

(A long choux pastry filled with cream and topped with chocolate.)

**Ingredients:**

- 1 batch choux pastry
- 1 cup pastry cream
- ½ cup chocolate ganache

**Instructions:**

1. Pipe and bake choux pastry into long strips.
2. Fill with pastry cream.
3. Dip tops in chocolate ganache and let set.

## Chouquette

(Small choux pastry balls topped with pearl sugar.)

**Ingredients:**

- 1 batch choux pastry
- ¼ cup pearl sugar

**Instructions:**

1. Pipe and bake small choux puffs.
2. Sprinkle with pearl sugar before baking.

## Profiterole

(Small choux pastries filled with ice cream and drizzled with chocolate.)

**Ingredients:**

- 1 batch choux pastry
- 2 cups vanilla ice cream
- ½ cup chocolate sauce

**Instructions:**

1. Pipe and bake small choux puffs.
2. Fill with ice cream.
3. Drizzle with chocolate sauce.

## Clafoutis

(A baked custard with cherries.)

**Ingredients:**

- 2 cups cherries, pitted
- 3 eggs
- ½ cup sugar
- ½ cup flour
- 1 cup milk
- 1 tsp vanilla

**Instructions:**

1. Preheat oven to 375°F (190°C). Butter a baking dish and add cherries.
2. Whisk eggs, sugar, flour, milk, and vanilla.
3. Pour over cherries and bake for 35-40 minutes.

## Crêpes Suzette

(Thin crêpes with orange sauce and flambéed.)

**Ingredients:**

**For the crêpes:**

- 1 cup flour
- 1 cup milk
- 2 eggs
- 1 tbsp butter, melted

**For the orange sauce:**

- ½ cup orange juice
- ¼ cup sugar
- 2 tbsp Grand Marnier (optional)
- 2 tbsp butter

**Instructions:**

1. Mix crêpe ingredients, let rest for 30 minutes, then cook thin crêpes.
2. Heat orange juice, sugar, and butter. Add Grand Marnier and flambé.
3. Coat crêpes in sauce and serve.

# Galette des Rois

(A traditional puff pastry filled with almond cream, eaten for Epiphany.)

**Ingredients:**

- 2 sheets puff pastry
- 1 egg (for egg wash)

**For the almond cream:**

- ½ cup butter, softened
- ½ cup sugar
- 1 cup almond flour
- 2 eggs
- 1 tsp vanilla extract

**Instructions:**

1. Preheat oven to 375°F (190°C).
2. Mix butter, sugar, almond flour, eggs, and vanilla until smooth.
3. Place one puff pastry sheet on a baking tray. Spread almond cream in the center, leaving a border.
4. Place the second sheet on top, seal edges, and brush with egg wash.
5. Score the top decoratively and bake for 30-35 minutes until golden.

## Pithivier

(A round puff pastry pie filled with frangipane or other fillings.)

**Ingredients:**

(Same as Galette des Rois)

**Instructions:**

1. Prepare almond cream as above.
2. Follow the same method as Galette des Rois but without the fève (small charm inside).

## Tarte au Citron Meringuée

(A lemon tart with a meringue topping.)

**Ingredients:**

**For the crust:**

- 1½ cups flour
- ½ cup butter
- ¼ cup sugar
- 1 egg

**For the lemon filling:**

- ½ cup lemon juice
- 1 tbsp lemon zest
- ½ cup sugar
- 3 eggs
- ½ cup butter

**For the meringue:**

- 2 egg whites
- ¼ cup sugar

**Instructions:**

1. Preheat oven to 350°F (175°C). Prepare and bake tart crust.
2. Cook lemon juice, zest, sugar, eggs, and butter until thick. Pour into crust.
3. Beat egg whites and sugar until stiff peaks form, then spread over tart.
4. Bake for 10 minutes until golden.

## Tarte aux Fraises

(A fresh strawberry tart with pastry cream.)

**Ingredients:**

**For the crust:** (Same as Tarte au Citron)
**For the pastry cream:**

- 1 cup milk
- 3 egg yolks
- ¼ cup sugar
- 2 tbsp cornstarch
- 1 tsp vanilla
  **For the topping:**
- 2 cups fresh strawberries

**Instructions:**

1. Prepare and bake tart crust.
2. Cook milk, yolks, sugar, and cornstarch until thick. Stir in vanilla.
3. Fill crust with pastry cream and top with strawberries.

## Tarte aux Pommes

(A classic French apple tart.)

**Ingredients:**

(Same as Tarte aux Fraises, replacing strawberries with sliced apples)

**Instructions:**

1. Arrange thinly sliced apples on top of the pastry cream.
2. Brush with apricot jam and bake at 375°F (190°C) for 30 minutes.

## Macaron

(French almond meringue cookies with a filling.)

**Ingredients:**

- 1 cup almond flour
- 1 cup powdered sugar
- 2 egg whites
- ¼ cup sugar
- Food coloring (optional)

**For the filling:**

- ½ cup buttercream or ganache

**Instructions:**

1. Whisk egg whites and sugar until stiff peaks form.
2. Fold in almond flour and powdered sugar.
3. Pipe small circles onto parchment paper and let rest for 30 minutes.
4. Bake at 300°F (150°C) for 12-15 minutes.
5. Fill with buttercream or ganache.

## Baba au Rhum

(A yeast cake soaked in rum syrup.)

### Ingredients:

- 1½ cups flour
- 1 tsp yeast
- 2 tbsp sugar
- 3 eggs
- ¼ cup butter
- ½ cup warm milk

### For the syrup:

- 1 cup sugar
- 1 cup water
- ½ cup rum

### Instructions:

1. Mix flour, yeast, sugar, eggs, butter, and milk. Let rise.
2. Bake in molds at 350°F (175°C) for 20 minutes.
3. Heat sugar and water, then add rum. Soak cakes in syrup.

## Gâteau Basque

(A Basque cake filled with pastry cream or jam.)

**Ingredients:**

- 1½ cups flour
- ½ cup butter
- ½ cup sugar
- 2 eggs
- 1 tsp vanilla
- 1 cup pastry cream

**Instructions:**

1. Mix flour, butter, sugar, eggs, and vanilla. Chill dough.
2. Roll half the dough into a tart pan, fill with pastry cream, and cover with the remaining dough.
3. Bake at 375°F (190°C) for 30-35 minutes.

## Pain d'Épices

(A French spice bread similar to gingerbread.)

**Ingredients:**

- 1 cup honey
- ½ cup sugar
- 2 cups flour
- 1 tsp baking soda
- 1 tsp cinnamon
- 1 tsp ginger
- ½ tsp cloves
- ½ cup milk

**Instructions:**

1. Preheat oven to 350°F (175°C).
2. Mix honey, sugar, flour, baking soda, and spices. Add milk.
3. Pour into a loaf pan and bake for 45 minutes.

# Gâteau Opéra

(A layered almond sponge cake with coffee buttercream and chocolate ganache.)

**Ingredients:**

**For the almond sponge (Joconde):**

- 6 egg whites
- 2 tbsp sugar
- 1 cup almond flour
- 1 cup powdered sugar
- 4 eggs
- ¼ cup flour
- 2 tbsp melted butter

**For the coffee syrup:**

- ½ cup water
- ¼ cup sugar
- 2 tbsp espresso

**For the coffee buttercream:**

- ½ cup sugar
- 2 tbsp water
- 2 egg yolks
- ½ cup butter, softened
- 1 tbsp espresso

**For the chocolate ganache:**

- ½ cup dark chocolate
- ¼ cup heavy cream

**Instructions:**

1. Preheat oven to 400°F (200°C). Prepare and bake Joconde sponge.
2. Simmer water, sugar, and espresso for syrup.
3. Make coffee buttercream by beating yolks while drizzling in sugar syrup, then adding butter and espresso.
4. Heat cream and mix with chocolate for ganache.
5. Assemble layers: sponge, syrup, buttercream, sponge, syrup, ganache, and repeat.

6. Chill before serving.

## Sablé Breton

(A rich, buttery shortbread from Brittany.)

**Ingredients:**

- 1 cup butter
- ½ cup sugar
- 2 egg yolks
- 2 cups flour
- 1 tsp baking powder
- 1 tsp salt

**Instructions:**

1. Cream butter and sugar, then add yolks.
2. Mix in flour, baking powder, and salt.
3. Roll out dough and cut into shapes.
4. Bake at 350°F (175°C) for 12-15 minutes.

## Tarte Tropézienne

(A brioche filled with pastry cream, made famous in Saint-Tropez.)

**Ingredients:**

**For the brioche:**

- 2½ cups flour
- ¼ cup sugar
- 1 tsp yeast
- 2 eggs
- ½ cup butter
- ¼ cup milk

**For the cream filling:**

- 1 cup milk
- 3 egg yolks
- ¼ cup sugar
- 2 tbsp cornstarch
- ½ cup whipped cream

**Instructions:**

1. Knead brioche dough, let rise, and bake at 350°F (175°C) for 25 minutes.
2. Make pastry cream, let cool, then fold in whipped cream.
3. Slice brioche in half and fill with cream.

## Mont Blanc

(A dessert made with sweet chestnut purée and whipped cream.)

**Ingredients:**

- 1 cup chestnut purée
- ½ cup sugar
- 1 tsp vanilla
- 1 cup whipped cream

**Instructions:**

1. Mix chestnut purée, sugar, and vanilla.
2. Pipe into nests and top with whipped cream.

# Fraisier

(A strawberry and cream cake.)

**Ingredients:**

**For the sponge cake:**

- 4 eggs
- ½ cup sugar
- ½ cup flour

**For the filling:**

- 1 cup pastry cream
- ½ cup whipped cream
- 2 cups fresh strawberries

**Instructions:**

1. Bake sponge cake.
2. Mix pastry cream and whipped cream.
3. Layer cake, cream, and strawberries.

## Croustade

(A flaky pastry tart, often filled with fruit.)

**Ingredients:**

- 2 cups flour
- ½ cup butter
- ¼ cup sugar
- ½ cup water
- 2 cups fruit (apples or pears)

**Instructions:**

1. Prepare pastry dough, roll out, and fill with fruit.
2. Bake at 375°F (190°C) for 35 minutes.

## Soufflé au Chocolat

(A classic French chocolate soufflé.)

**Ingredients:**

- 3 tbsp butter
- 3 tbsp flour
- 1 cup milk
- ½ cup dark chocolate
- 3 egg yolks
- 4 egg whites
- ¼ cup sugar

**Instructions:**

1. Make a roux with butter and flour, add milk, then stir in chocolate.
2. Mix in egg yolks.
3. Beat egg whites and sugar, fold into mixture.
4. Bake at 375°F (190°C) for 12 minutes.

## Flan Parisien

(A creamy baked custard tart.)

**Ingredients:**

- 1 pie crust
- 2 cups milk
- ½ cup sugar
- 3 egg yolks
- ¼ cup cornstarch
- 1 tsp vanilla

**Instructions:**

1. Bake pie crust.
2. Cook milk, sugar, yolks, cornstarch, and vanilla until thick.
3. Pour into crust and bake at 375°F (190°C) for 35 minutes.

## Charlotte aux Fraises

(A no-bake dessert with ladyfingers and strawberry cream.)

**Ingredients:**

- 20 ladyfingers
- 2 cups strawberries
- ½ cup sugar
- 1 cup whipped cream

**Instructions:**

1. Line a mold with ladyfingers.
2. Blend strawberries and sugar, mix with whipped cream.
3. Fill mold and chill overnight.

## Bûche de Noël

(A traditional Christmas Yule log cake.)

**Ingredients:**

**For the sponge cake:**

- 4 eggs
- ½ cup sugar
- ½ cup flour
- 2 tbsp cocoa powder
- 1 tsp baking powder

**For the filling:**

- 1 cup whipped cream
- ½ cup chocolate ganache

**For the frosting:**

- 1 cup butter
- ½ cup cocoa powder
- 2 cups powdered sugar
- 2 tbsp milk

**Instructions:**

1. Bake sponge cake, roll while warm, then unroll.
2. Spread with whipped cream and ganache, then roll back.
3. Cover with frosting, create bark texture, and decorate.

## Puits d'Amour

(A puff pastry filled with caramelized pastry cream.)

**Ingredients:**

- 1 sheet puff pastry
- 1 cup pastry cream
- ½ cup caramel sauce

**Instructions:**

1. Cut and bake pastry rounds.
2. Fill with pastry cream and top with caramel.

# Gâteau Mille-Crêpes

(A layered crepe cake with pastry cream.)

**Ingredients:**

**For the crêpes:**

- 2 cups milk
- 4 eggs
- 1 cup flour
- 2 tbsp butter
- 2 tbsp sugar

**For the filling:**

- 2 cups pastry cream
- 1 cup whipped cream

**Instructions:**

1. Make crêpes and chill.
2. Layer crêpes with pastry cream.
3. Chill before serving.

## Merveilleux

(A delicate meringue sandwich coated in whipped cream and chocolate.)

**Ingredients:**

- 3 egg whites
- ½ cup sugar
- 1 cup whipped cream
- ½ cup chocolate shavings

**Instructions:**

1. Bake small meringue discs.
2. Sandwich with whipped cream and coat in chocolate shavings.

## Nougat de Montélimar

(A chewy almond and honey nougat from Provence.)

**Ingredients:**

- 1 cup honey
- ½ cup sugar
- 1 egg white
- 1 cup almonds
- ½ cup pistachios

**Instructions:**

1. Heat honey and sugar to 250°F (120°C).
2. Beat egg white and slowly add syrup.
3. Mix in nuts and pour into a mold.

## Quatre-Quarts

(A classic French pound cake.)

### Ingredients:

- 1 cup flour
- 1 cup sugar
- 1 cup butter
- 4 eggs

### Instructions:

1. Beat eggs and sugar, add butter and flour.
2. Bake at 350°F (175°C) for 40 minutes.

## Pain aux Raisins

(A flaky pastry with custard and raisins.)

**Ingredients:**

- 1 sheet puff pastry
- ½ cup pastry cream
- ½ cup raisins

**Instructions:**

1. Spread pastry cream over dough, add raisins.
2. Roll, slice, and bake at 375°F (190°C) for 15 minutes.

## Beignet

(A deep-fried French doughnut.)

**Ingredients:**

- 2 cups flour
- 2 tbsp sugar
- 1 tsp yeast
- ½ cup milk
- 1 egg
- Oil for frying

**Instructions:**

1. Knead dough, let rise, then roll and cut.
2. Fry until golden and dust with sugar.

## Gâteau Breton

(A dense butter cake from Brittany.)

**Ingredients:**

- 2 cups flour
- 1 cup sugar
- 1 cup butter
- 4 egg yolks

**Instructions:**

1. Mix ingredients into dough.
2. Bake at 350°F (175°C) for 35 minutes.

## Fougasse Sucrée

(A sweet version of the traditional Provençal bread.)

**Ingredients:**

- 2 cups flour
- ½ cup sugar
- 1 tsp yeast
- ½ cup milk
- ¼ cup butter

**Instructions:**

1. Knead dough, let rise, then shape.
2. Bake at 375°F (190°C) for 20 minutes.

## Gâteau de Savoie

(A light sponge cake from the Alps.)

**Ingredients:**

- 4 eggs
- ½ cup sugar
- ½ cup flour
- 1 tsp baking powder

**Instructions:**

1. Beat eggs and sugar, fold in flour.
2. Bake at 350°F (175°C) for 25 minutes.

## Tourtière

(A savory meat pie from Quebec.)

**Ingredients:**

- 1 lb ground pork
- 1 onion, chopped
- ½ cup mashed potatoes
- 1 tsp cinnamon
- 1 pie crust

**Instructions:**

1. Cook pork with onion and spices.
2. Mix with potatoes, fill crust, and bake at 375°F (190°C) for 30 minutes.

www.ingramcontent.com/pod-product-compliance
Lightning Source LLC
LaVergne TN
LVHW081325060526
838201LV00055B/2465